THE RULES OF ENGAGEMENT
MINI

If you live long enough you will come across a problem that money, contacts, or medicine cannot solve. Only the knowledge of the *The Rules of Engagement* can save you.

★ ★

KAKRA BAIDEN

Copyright © 2017 by Kakra Baiden
Published by Airpower Publications

The Rules of Engagement Mini
by Kakra Baiden

Printed in the United States of America

ISBN: 978-1-945123-80-1

All rights reserved under international copyright law. Written permission must be secured from the publisher to use or reproduce any part of this book except for brief quotations in critical reviews or articles.

Scripture quotations are taken from the King James Version of the Bible.

The author has added italics in Scripture and text for emphasis.

E-mail: info@kakrabaiden.org

Contents

The Rules of Engagement...5

Understanding the Rules of Engagement...8

The Rule of Relationships...16

The Rule of Favour...24

The Rule of Faith...29

The Rule of Mercy...32

The Rule of Love...39

The Rule of the Name of Jesus...46

The White Horse...62

The Rules of Engagement

Over the years I have seen my prayer life improve and the power behind my prayer strengthen. Demons it took hours to cast out now come out in minutes. Answers to prayer that took days are now secured within minutes. I have seen God perform outstanding miracles through prayer.

If God cannot change, then I am the one who has changed. I believe this change has come about because over time my understanding of the rules of engagement concerning prayer has increased.

WHAT ARE THE RULES OF ENGAGEMENT?

The word "engagement" is usually related to marriage, but it also means a battle between two opposing armies. "Rules of engagement" means the rules that govern a battle or fight.

For though we walk in the flesh, we do not *war* after the flesh: (For the weapons of our warfare are not carnal, but mighty through God to the pulling down of strong holds) (2 Cor. 10:3-4).

Whether or not you are aware, the Bible tells us that we are in a war. Our battle is not a physical one but a spiritual one, and our main enemy is the devil.

My prayers have become more effective and powerful than before because my understanding of the rules of prayer has improved over time. This has affected my prayer life tremendously and is the reason I can now pray more effectively.

A Deformed Leg Restored

One day I received a call from a church member whose wife had just delivered a baby girl with a deformed leg. After praying, the deformed leg remained the same.

About an hour after we had left the ward, we heard screams. We went back into the ward to find that the deformed leg had been replaced by a perfect, brand new leg.

I saw the power of God! This tells you the power of prayer.

TEACH US TO PRAY

The Prayer Life of Jesus

Jesus had a powerful and effective prayer life. He was found praying many times in the Bible.

And in the morning, rising up a great while before day, he went out, and departed into a solitary place, and there *prayed* (Mark 1:35).

One day, the disciples of Jesus approached Him concerning their ineffective prayers. Luke 11:1 states, "It came to pass, that, as he was praying in a certain place, when he ceased, one of his disciples said unto him, Lord, *teach us to pray*, as John also taught his disciples."

They had come to the realization that the mere act of praying was not sufficient for answered prayer.

What made the prayer life of Jesus so powerful? It is simple! He understood the "rules of engagement."

Understanding the Rules of Engagement

He that turneth away his ear from *hearing the law*, even his prayer shall be abomination (Prov. 28:9).

The word "law" means rules, and the word "abomination" means disgusting.

I would like to rephrase this verse to make the meaning clearer. "Prayer is based on laws or rules and the man who does not observe these laws will pray all right, but it will be disgusting before the Lord."

MISCONCEPTIONS ABOUT PRAYER

And when thou prayest, thou shalt not be as the hypocrites [are]: for they love to pray standing in the synagogues and in the corners of the streets, that they may be seen of men. Verily I say unto you, They have their reward. But thou, when thou prayest, enter into thy closet, and when thou hast shut thy door, pray to thy Father which is in secret; and thy Father which seeth in secret shall reward thee openly. But when ye pray, use not vain repetitions, as the heathen [do]: for they think that they shall be heard for their much speaking (Matt. 6:5-7).

"Misconception" simply means something that is not properly understood. Here are a few misconceptions about prayer.

Answered Prayer Is Not Based on Your Geographical Location

...they love to pray in the *synagogues* and the *corners of the streets* (Matt. 6:5).

The Pharisees loved to pray in specific places: the synagogues and the corners of the streets. To them, location was a big part of their prayer life.

There are people who believe that unless they pray at particular locations, God will not hear their prayers. It could be a church building, a field, a room, or a place where they may have had some special or supernatural experience.

Imagine you have a gun that only works in your house. A real gun should be able to work in all locations: on the street, in the kitchen, in a mall, and even in the bathroom.

Jesus prayed everywhere: on the mountain, at sea, at a wedding, on the streets, people's homes, and while walking on the road. In fact, many of Jesus' miracles occurred outside the church.

One day someone called me from South Africa for prayer. After praying, the line went dead. After some seconds I heard the voice again. When

I asked the person why there was a break, she answered, "I fell under the power."

The power of God went through the phone and knocked her over. All this happened while I was eating in my dining room. May you perform miracles while you are eating!

The Woman at the Well

In John 4 the Bible talks about a woman Jesus engaged in a conversation. The woman said,

> Our fathers worshipped in this mountain; and ye say, that in Jerusalem is the place where men ought to worship. Jesus saith unto her, Woman, believe me, the hour cometh, when ye shall neither in this mountain, nor yet at Jerusalem, worship the Father (John 4:20-21).
>
> But the hour cometh, and now is, when the true worshippers shall worship the Father in *spirit* and in *truth*: for the Father seeketh such to worship him (John 4:23).

Prayer is driven by *truth*, the principles of the *Word of God,* and *the leading of the Spirit.* That is what makes prayer effective.

Answered Prayer Is Not Necessarily Based on Lengthy Prayers

But when ye pray, use not vain repetitions, as the heathen [do]: for they think that they shall be heard for their *much speaking* (Matt. 6:7).

Lengthy prayer is and can be necessary, but it does not necessarily guarantee answered prayer. Jesus Himself used to pray for long periods of time.

There are people who assume that because they have been for an all-night prayer meeting it means their prayers have been answered. They become frustrated when they do not see any results. Nothing could be further from the truth.

Sometimes empty heads and hearts who may not have even read their Bibles the whole year assume that the passage of time alone guarantees answered prayer. Many people who are like that unfortunately have very little success in prayer.

In the book of Isaiah the Bible records God's response to the lengthy prayers of Israel, "And when ye spread forth your hands, I will hide mine eyes from you: yea, when ye make many prayers, I will not hear: your hands are full of blood" (Isa.1:15). They made "many prayers," thinking it would bring them answers, but God told them to "Learn to do well..." (Isa. 1:17).

Their problem was ignorance; they had not learned the "rules of engagement."

The Woman Who Suffered from Schizophrenia

One day I received a call from one of my pastors who said that a certain woman suffering from schizophrenia had been brought to the church for prayer. I decided to rest for a while before going for the all-night prayer meeting.

In my sleep, the Lord appeared to me and said, "Effective prayer is not just based on how long you pray. When you meet that sick woman, do not pray for more than one minute or I will not listen to your prayers. Just command the spirit to leave and I will do it."

Later when I got to the church I met the woman and her family waiting anxiously for me. I laid my hands on her and said, "In the name of Jesus, I release you from any demonic power that hinders your mind. Amen!" I turned to her family members and announced, "She is healed!"

They looked at me in disbelief and asked, "Ah, Pastor, is that all?" I could tell from their faces that they were confused. Why? Because they had associated effective prayer with long prayers.

They called me after three days with joy and told me they had observed her for the past three days and she had truly been healed.

Answered Prayer Is Not Based on the Volume of Your Voice

Whether you pray loudly or silently has no bearing on answered prayer unless it is by the influence of the Holy Spirit. Some people equate power in prayer with the volume of their voice. God is neither deaf nor nervous. Hebrews 5:7 describes the prayer of Jesus in the garden of Gethsemane:

Who in the days of his flesh, when he had offered up prayers and supplications with *strong crying* and *tears* unto him that was able to save him from death, and was *heard* in that he *feared* (Heb. 5:7).

However, I would like to point out that Jesus was not heard because of the tears, strong crying, or sweat. He was "heard in that *He feared.*"

Similarly, if you sit silently like a monk, it also does not mean that God will answer your prayers.

Silent Prayer Can Produce Results

Hannah prayed to God for a child and because there was no sound, Eli thought Hannah was drunk. Regardless of the silence, it was a prayer that moved heaven.

Now Hannah, she *spake in her heart*; only *her lips moved*, but *her voice was not heard*: therefore Eli thought she had been drunken (1 Sam. 1:13).

Loud Prayer Can Produce Results

And when he thus had spoken, he cried with *a loud voice*, Lazarus, come forth. And he that was dead came forth, bound hand and foot with graveclothes: and his face was bound about with a napkin. Jesus saith unto them, Loose him, and let him go (John 11:43-44).

At the raising of Lazarus, Jesus raised His voice and commanded the dead man to come out and Lazarus was instantly raised from the dead. There is a place for shouting in prayer and shouting can sometimes raise the dead. Amen!

Answered Prayer Is Not Entirely Based on Fasting

Moreover when ye *fast*, be not, as the hypocrites, of a sad countenance: for they disfigure their faces, that they may appear unto men to fast. Verily I say unto you, They have their reward (Matt. 6:16).

Fasting is very good, but it must be governed by the rules of engagement. Many fast but are not aware that they are actually on a hunger strike.

Isaiah 58 talks about a group who fasted for some time but still had no answer.

They made the dangerous assumption that once they were on a fast, their prayers were getting to heaven. If it was so, then God would have to answer the prayer of witches who are on a fast!

...ye shall not fast as [ye do this] day, to make your voice to be heard on high" (Isa. 58:3-4).

He Is Supposed to Divorce His Wife and Marry Me

One day a certain lady told me someone's husband was supposed to marry her. Therefore she was embarking on a fast.

There are some who hatch wicked plans and try to force God to endorse them through fasting and prayer.

The Rule of Relationships

FATHER-SON RELATIONSHIP

Answered prayer is determined by the law of relationships. One day a certain young woman told me how she had given her ex-boyfriend thousands of dollars as a loan without collateral. When the relationship ended, she could not retrieve her money since there was no evidence. She was ready and willing to part with her savings because of the relationship that existed between them.

THE FOUNDATION OF ANSWERED PRAYER

In Matthew 6:9, Jesus taught that the foundation or bedrock of answered prayer is our *relationship* with God.

After this manner therefore pray ye: *Our Father* which art in heaven, Hallowed be thy name. Thy kingdom come (Matt. 6:9-10a).

Jesus said when you pray, say, "*our Father.*" The word "father" represents the highest relationship.

Our relationship with God is the foundation on which all prayer rests. All the promises in the Lord's Prayer, like, "Give us our daily bread," and "Deliver us from evil," are all determined by this relationship; the father-son relationship.

Men at Work!

One day whilst driving my daughter home from school I came across a beggar by the roadside, hoping to receive some tips from the passing motorists. Some people totally ignored him and others threw coins at him.

Before we got home, my daughter said in her sweet little voice, "Daddy, I want you to buy me some sweets." I drove to a nearby shop and bought her sweets, plus other things she had not asked for.

My daughter did not need to beg or work for the sweets because of the relationship that exists between us. She is my darling daughter and I am her daddy, period! I was willing to do exceedingly and abundantly above all that she could ask for or even think of.

A Good Relationship Counts

And he that sent me is with me: the *Father* hath not left me alone; for I do always those things that please him (John 8:29).

There are children of God who have a very bad relationship with their heavenly Father. This tends to rob them of their inheritance in Christ. Some Christians have unanswered prayers because of the bad relationship they have with their heavenly Father.

The Unscrupulous Businessman

Years ago I visited the workshop of a businessman who was supposed to manufacture some furniture for us. We had already pre-financed it. I was told he was on a twenty-one-day fast, so I could not see him. I said, "This man must be a very spiritual person." Later I came to discover that he was a first-class liar and cheat because he tried to swindle us. I started wondering, "How can someone who prays and fasts for twenty-one days be so dishonest and such a big liar?"

The Rule of Relationships Raised the Dead

I don't know if you are familiar with the story of Lazarus. He had been dead for four days, but Jesus raised him from the dead.

The faith and confidence of Jesus that the dead man would be raised was drawn from the law of relationships. Jesus lifted up His eyes to heaven and said, "Father." He reminded Him of their relationship. He drew on His relationship with God to raise Lazarus.

It reminds me of my own little daughter, Chloe. When she lifts up those cute eyes to look into my eyes and says, "Daddy, I need an ice cream," something just breaks in my heart. When my kids ask me for something legitimate, I find it hard to say no! The moment I hear that magical word, "Daddy," they charm me. They rely on the power of relationships to get me to answer their prayer, not hard work.

The Rule of Relationships Opens the Heavens

Now when all the people were baptized, it came to pass, that Jesus also being baptized, and praying, the heaven was opened, And the Holy Ghost descended in a bodily shape like a dove upon him, and a voice came from heaven, which said, Thou art my beloved Son; in thee I am well pleased (Luke 3:21-22).

The Heavens Opened Over My Life

I remember once praying and fasting for some days and seeking the fellowship of the Holy Spirit. On the fifth day of my fast, around three in the morning, I heard an audible voice call my name three times in the room: "Kakra, Kakra, Kakra."

I shouted with joy, "Holy Spirit!" That day, the heavens had opened over my life. It was one of the most joyous experiences of my life.

The reason God manifested Himself at the baptism of Jesus was because of the law of relationships. He said, "This is my beloved Son." It was not primarily because of the fasting, prayer, or even the baptism. It was because of sonship.

RELATIONSHIP WITH FELLOW HUMANS

Apart from our relationship with Christ, our relationship with fellow humans also greatly influences prayer. I would like us to examine three of these relationships.

1. The Relationship Between You and Your Spouse

That Your Prayers Be Not Hindered

Likewise, ye husbands, dwell with them according to knowledge, giving honour unto the wife, as unto the weaker vessel, and as being *heirs together* of the grace of life; that your *prayers be not hindered* (1 Peter 3:7).

Husbands are supposed to dwell with their wives according to knowledge. What specific knowledge is this? It is the knowledge that without a good relationship with your spouse, your prayers will be hindered. It is amazing how God places great emphasis on relationships and prayer.

JOINT SIGNATORIES

My wife and I keep our money together. We are joint signatories to the same accounts. In marriage, you become a joint signatory with your partner to a "joint spiritual account" that has been created in heaven for you. There is a bank in heaven that supplies our needs when we pray.

The interesting thing to note here is that to access this account you will need the signature of your spouse, who is your co-signatory to the account, otherwise the cheque cannot be cashed. Your prayers will be hindered.

God Started Laughing

I remember once having a serious disagreement with my wife. Out of anger I went into my study to pray and wait on the Lord. When I began praying, it was as if I could hear God laughing. The Holy Spirit said to me, "Don't waste your time. Reconcile with your wife before you talk to Me."

The Final Conclusion

Finally, Peter concludes by saying, "For the eyes of the Lord [are] over the righteous and his ears [are open] *unto their prayers*: but the face of the Lord [is] against them that do evil" (1 Peter 3:12). God is watching your relationship with your spouse more than your sanctimonious prayers in the church.

If you hold something against your spouse, it is time to let it go because greater issues are at stake; your whole prayer life is at stake.

2. Your Relationship between Your Fellow Brothers and Sisters in Christ

Therefore if thou bring thy gift to the altar, and there rememberest that *thy brother hath ought against thee*; *leave* there thy gift before the altar, and *go* thy way; first be *reconciled to thy brother* (Matt. 5:23-24).

This Scripture talks about how to give an offering as a gift to God. It could be an offering of money, praise, or worship.

God values relationships between fellow believers more than prayer and offerings.

There are many people giving to churches but not to God. They have many grudges with their fellow brothers and sisters yet still give offerings to God. God's verdict is final; He will reject it if you have something against your brother.

Vision of Unforgiveness

One day I had a misunderstanding with a fellow Christian brother, and like we sometimes do, I said to myself, *I have forgiven him, but I will not have anything to do with him.* That night I had a very vivid vision that showed my spiritual condition.

I had been imprisoned with very hardened criminals. Eventually an angel appeared and said, "We know you are a pastor, but God has cast you away from His presence because you refused to forgive brother so-and-so."

I was shocked to discover bitterness and unforgiveness had taken me away from the presence of God. How were my prayers going to be answered? I repented and asked for forgiveness.

3. Your Relationship with the Weak

Whoso stoppeth his ears at the cry of the poor, he also shall cry himself, but shall not be heard (Prov. 21:13).

When you look at the ministry of Jesus, you will realize that He really cared for the poor and weak. No wonder He had a powerful prayer life.

The Rule of Favour

The word "favour" means to be kind or partial to someone. I have four children. Sometimes what I do for them partly depends on the level of favour they have in my eyes. The older ones know that their youngest sister has more favour in my eyes because of her age. Because of this the rest of my children try to use her to obtain favours from me.

One day I was in my room when she came and said, "Daddy, I want to tell you something."

Judging from the conversation, I gathered one of her siblings had sent her.

I looked at her and asked, "Who sent you?"

She looked at me innocently and said, "Caleb sent me."

Caleb is my eldest son and he knows that favour is important if his requests are going to be granted.

Jesus Enjoyed the Favour of God

In John 11:21-22, Martha said, "Lord, if thou hadst been here, my brother had not died. But *I know, that even now, whatsoever thou wilt ask of God, God will give [it] to thee.*"

Martha said, "You have favour before God that we don't have. I asked God to bring my brother to life, but nothing happened. As for You, I know God will hear Your prayer, because You have favour in His sight."

YOU CAN GROW IN FAVOUR

Did you know that you can grow in favour? Jesus was born with some measure of favour, but He consciously increased the level of favour upon His life.

And Jesus *increased* in wisdom and stature, and in *favour* with God and man (Luke 2:52).

HOW TO WIN FAVOUR

He that sent me is with me: the *Father* hath not left me alone; for I *do always* those *things* that *please* him (John 8:29).

I know the things that please my wife and I sometimes do those things to win favours from her. I know what I have to do, especially when night approaches. Similarly, there are certain things that please God and win His favour.
Jesus said, "I know exactly what to do to win my Father's favour, and I do those things always." Not sometimes, but always.

To attract the favour of God, we must learn to do the things that please Him. What are these things?

1. Holiness

Jesus Pleased God Because He Was Holy

Now when all the people were baptized, it came to pass, that Jesus also being baptized, and praying, the heaven was opened, And the Holy Ghost descended in a bodily shape like a dove upon him, and a voice came from heaven, which said, Thou art my beloved Son; in thee I am *well pleased* (Luke 3:21-22).

I ask myself, *What had Jesus done up to this point to win the favour of God?* At this time He had not fasted for forty days, He had not started preaching, and He had not healed or converted anyone, but God was so pleased with Him. What could be the reason? The reason is simple: holiness.

Jesus had the nature of the lamb, a symbol of purity and holiness; that was why the Lord was pleased with Him.

Many people have substituted holiness for religion. The word "religion" means what you do for God. They have sown fig leaves to cover their nakedness. They jump from prophet to prophet, man of God to man of God, church to church, and prayer meeting to prayer meeting. Sometimes all of these things are done to camouflage our disobedience. All you need to do is be holy, and when you whisper, heaven will hear.

2. The Fear of God

He will fulfil the *desire* of them that *fear him*; he also will *hear their cry*, and will save them (Ps. 145:19).

Then they that *feared* the *Lord* spake often one to another: and the *Lord harkened*, and heard [it], and a book of remembrance was written before him for them that *feared* the *Lord*, and that thought upon his name (Mal. 3:16).

When you fear God, even your casual conversation becomes like a prayer unto God. I have seen it many times in my own life when something I said in a casual conversation manifested as an answered prayer.

My Faulty Phone Was Replaced

Some time ago I used to have a nice phone which I really liked, but it suddenly developed a problem. That same day while I was in conversation with one of our pastors, I said, "This phone is not good. I have to change it and get a new one."

The following day a brother came to me and said, "Prophet, I just thought I should bring you this gift." When I opened it, it was the latest model of my faulty phone. God had listened to my conversation and responded to my comment.

The Rule of Faith

To win the favour of God you must be a man of faith because faith pleases God. Recently I was preaching at a conference when I saw a woman lying motionless in front of the stage. The Spirit of God said to me, "I am ready to heal that woman if you can believe it."

I said, "Lord, I believe."

The Holy Spirit said to me, "Now tell them she is going to walk and after she is going to dance."

I boldly said it and asked for the woman to be brought to me. I made her relatives prop her up in an upright position and then I held her hand and said to the people supporting her, "Now everyone back off."

When they left go of her, the paralyzed woman now stood unaided. I pulled her toward me and started walking with her. At first her steps were short and unsteady, but with each step her gait became firmer and stronger than previously. By the time we reached one end of the stage, I let her go, and she started walking by herself, and finally, she started dancing by herself. Jesus healed her! Faith had won the favour of God.

THE WILL OF GOD

In Luke 22:42, Jesus said, "Father, if thou be willing, remove this cup from me: nevertheless *not my will*, but *thine*, be done." One way to win the favour of God is to do His will.

Most firms give bonuses at the end or the beginning of the year. This bonus may vary in size, depending on the level of the employee or the contribution of the employee. When employees follow the "will of the company" and excel in their given area they win the favour of the company and it makes them enjoy a bonus.

The word "will" means the capacity to take decisions. God has left the capacity to make decisions in the hands of every man. When we choose the will of God, it pleases Him and wins His favour.

My Children Did Not Obey My Will

One day my wife and I went out in the evening. When we came back our kids were still not asleep. They had taken advantage of our absence to go against our will. They were jumping and playing around, knowing full well it was past their bedtime. I was angry and drove them to sleep.

After a while, my little daughter, who always enjoys favour in my eyes, came and said, "Daddy, I want to eat."

I said to her, "You will not eat. Go and sleep."

At that point she had lost favour before me because she had disobeyed my will. Because of that her request was denied. If you go against the will of God, you will lose favour.

And this is the *confidence* that we have in him, that, if we ask any thing according to his will, he heareth us: And if we know that he hear us, whatsoever we ask, we know that we have the petitions that we desired of him (1 John 5:14-15).

I remember when I was in my teens. Any time I went against my dad's will by disobeying him, I became fearful when he came home. I would stay far away from him and would not dare ask him for any favour, like using his car, because I knew I had done something wrong. People who go against the will of God will be fearful and stay far away from Him.

The Rule of Mercy

GOD IS MERCIFUL

And the *Lord* passed by before him, and proclaimed, The *Lord*, The *Lord* God, *merciful* and gracious, longsuffering, and abundant in goodness and truth, Keeping mercy for thousands, forgiving iniquity and transgression and sin, and that will by no means clear [the guilty]; visiting the iniquity of the fathers upon the children, and upon the children's children, unto the third and to the fourth [generation] (Ex. 34: 6-7).

God revealed his nature to Moses. In summary, God told Moses, "I have two sides. I am a *merciful God*, but I am also a *judge*."

You Must Understand That God Is Merciful

An understanding of the mercy of God is very important if you are to have a powerful prayer life. "Why?" you may ask. Because anytime you pray you will have a feeling of inadequacy. A feeling that there is something you were supposed to have done that you did not do. This can undermine your faith and will in turn cause you to lack boldness and faith in prayer.

What can take away this feeling of unbelief, inadequacy, and guilt? The knowledge of the nature of God! That God is a merciful God!

A Vision Concerning the Mercy of God

One day I had a vision and found myself before the throne of God. A film of someone's life was being played on a large screen. The man in this film was engaged in sinful activities like beating and cheating people, fornicating, lying, drunkenness, etc. I wondered how someone could do all those things in the full view of God. I could not see the face of this bad man, though; I only saw his back.

As the film progressed, I wondered, *Who is this bad man?* Finally the man turned around. Guess who I saw? It was *me!*

Although I was not physically involved in such things, God was showing me the state of my heart and spirit.

To my surprise the Lord spoke and said, "Promote this man." I did not deserve it because I was a sinful man.

I thought, *What kind of promotion is this?* It was then I realized I was standing at the throne of grace. I was not only pardoned, but I was also promoted; not because of my works, but because of His mercy.

YOUR PERSPECTIVE ABOUT JESUS IS VERY IMPORTANT

The word "perspective" means how you see things. It is important how you see problems. Every problem could be an opportunity depending on how you see it.

When David saw Goliath, he saw an opportunity: a pretty girl, money, and freedom from paying taxes. When the soldiers saw Goliath, they saw their blood on the streets and ran away. How do you see Jesus?

THE GREAT HIGH PRIEST—JESUS

Seeing then that we have *a great high priest*, that is passed into the *heavens, Jesus the Son of God*, let us hold fast [our] profession. For we have not an high priest which cannot be touched with the feeling of our infirmities; but was in all points *tempted like as we are*, yet without sin. Let us therefore come boldly unto the throne of grace, that we may obtain mercy, and find grace to help in time of need (Heb. 4:14-16).

This Scripture starts with the word "seeing," which also means "perspective." Your perspective of Jesus is very important if you are to relate to Him well in prayer.

He Is Our Lawyer

Jesus is in heaven, representing us and pleading our case. Therefore it is important to see Jesus as your lawyer, interceding for you—not against you.

The Son of God—He Is Influential

Apart from Him being the high priest, He is also a very influential person in heaven. He is not just an ordinary person; He is the Son of God.

One day a woman who wanted me to pray for her decided to pass her request through my four-year-old daughter.

I immediately kneeled down and prayed for her teacher.

When we pass our requests through the Son of God, we can be assured God will get the message right there in His "bedroom."

He Has a Strategic Position

Jesus is not only a son; He is also seated at a strategic position: the right hand of God. He is seated right by Him. Even if He whispers, God will hear it.

He Empathizes with Us

For we have not an high priest which cannot be touched with the feeling of our infirmities; but was in all points *tempted like as* [*we are*, yet] without sin (Heb. 4:15).

There is a difference between *empathy* and *sympathy*. The word "sympathy" means to show sorrow, grief, or concern to someone. The word "empathy" means to show sorrow, grief, or concern to someone because you have experienced what he or she is going through.

It is always easy to relate to people who have been through your experience because they are more understanding and caring. Novices, on the other hand, may not appreciate and understand your situation.

THE MERCY OF GOD

Let us therefore come boldly unto the throne of grace, that we may obtain mercy, and find grace to help in time of need (Heb. 4:16).

Sometimes when people do not come to church I know they are purging themselves. Some stay at home for two weeks until they feel holy enough to come back to church. They come back only when they feel forgiven.

The Rule of Mercy

Forgiveness is not a feeling; it is based on the integrity of God's Word. You do not have to feel forgiven; you must know you are forgiven if you have repented and asked for forgiveness. Jesus sits on a throne of grace, not justice.

One day I went to preach outside the country. On our way to the service, I told the pastor, "I feel hungry. I need to go back and eat." Afterwards we went into the service and I preached powerfully, with miracles and signs following.

After the service, the pastor asked, "Prophet, I was very surprised when you ate. I thought you would be fasting and praying before you get there."

I turned to him and said, "I do not rely on fasting and prayers as my cardinal key. My cardinal key is the mercy of God."

I want to share with you a letter from an unbeliever who was miraculously healed in a miracle service.

Healed of Liver Failure!

Dear Prophet,

My health was retiring and I was sinking daily. I couldn't tell what was wrong.

A colleague in the office told me of the drastic change in my complexion and loss of weight.

Finally I was diagnosed with liver inflammation. This meant I was losing the enzymes in my liver. My whole life came to a halt. What could I do when I had just been made aware of how close I was to losing my life? The doctor became so concerned. He thought I was too young for that.

He demanded I took a "bed rest." Two days later, you had your conference.

My sister and mum thought the convention was timely. They challenged me to dare *God*. I disobeyed clinical advice and attended the convention.

Three days after the convention, I mentioned to my doctor that I was healed. He didn't believe it.

He asked me to do further tests at three different laboratories to prove it. I picked up the results and they all proved my liver was all right.

I have since had a reason to believe in *God* through Jesus Christ the Son!

The Rule of Love

"He Ripped Me Off"

One day I met a stranger at an airport and she said, "Prophet, so good to see you. You do not know me, but I have a problem I would like to discuss with you." I decided to give her some of my time.

She continued, "I have this boyfriend who has taken a huge amount of money from me and broken the relationship."

I asked her why she gave out such a huge amount of money to him.

She replied, "You know, Prophet, I loved him, and so based on that, he started borrowing money from me. I realize he exploited me because he knew I would do anything for him." She continued, "For this reason, he ripped me off."

Similarly, if you know how much God loves you, you can "rip Him off!"

He that spared not his own Son, but delivered him up for us all, how shall he not with him also *freely give* us all things? (Rom. 8:32).

Delilah knew Samson loved her and that was why she was able to make him tell her the source of his strength.

THE NATURE OF LOVE

Set me *as a seal upon thine heart*, as *a seal upon thine arm*: for *love [is] strong as death*; jealousy [is] cruel as the grave: the coals thereof [are] coals of fire, [which hath a] most vehement flame (Song of Solomon 8:6).

Love Is Tangible

This verse describes the nature of love. When you love someone, you want to make it visible. Love always wants to be worn as a seal on the arm. Therefore it is impossible to say you love someone and not express it tangibly.

God also makes His love tangible to us by responding to our prayer.

Healed of a Spinal Problem

Just this afternoon I saw God respond to my prayer in love. A woman with a spinal problem who could not walk was brought to me by her children for prayer. I laid my hands on her and prayed for Jesus to heal her.

A noise like a gust of wind escaped out of her lips. Suddenly she started shouting, "I am healed! I am healed!" She jumped up from the chair and started walking to the glory of God. The love of God found her and healed her!

Love Is As Strong As Death

The power of love is as strong as the power of death. I remember when my father died. At his funeral, he would not respond to anything.

When people fall deeply in love, they can sometimes behave like dead people. No amount of talking, advice, or counsel can stop them from breaking up a bad relationship. They become "dead in love" and do not respond to any external influence.

When you grasp the depth of God's love, no amount of guilt the devil will throw your way can undermine your faith. May God bless you contrary to people's protestations!

Love Can Make You Give All Your Substance

Song of Solomon 8:7 says, "Many waters cannot quench love, neither can the floods drown it: if a man would *give* all the substance of his house for love, it would utterly be contemned."

There was a friend of mine who fell helplessly in love with a certain lady. Within a matter of days he had made the lady a co-owner of his company. I was shocked! Meanwhile, I had known him for years, but he had never given me anything substantial. What made him do this? It was love!

Because God loves us, He is ready to give everything, including His Son. "For God so *loved* the world, that *he gave* his only begotten Son, that whosoever believeth in him should not perish, but have everlasting life" (John 3:16).

WE ARE SUSPICIOUS ABOUT THE LOVE OF GOD

And to know the love of Christ, which passeth knowledge, that ye might be filled with all the fulness of God (Eph. 3:19).

Many years ago, whilst walking with a certain young man I knew, we ran into a girl we knew in the neighborhood. My friend invited her to a party he was organizing. This was her reply.
She said, "Ei, Joe, I know you. I think you have evil intentions toward me."
The girl doubted the sincerity of the invitation; she thought the invitation had an ulterior motive.
We usually doubt the love of God and think there must be an ulterior motive when He invites us to serve Him.
Surely this love cannot be understood. That is why it takes revelation.

The Hardcore Unbeliever

One day I witnessed to a hardcore unbeliever gentleman who gave his life to Christ. The following day I went to visit him and found him in bed with his girlfriend. I took him outside and asked him why he wanted to go back to his old lifestyle.

He looked at me and said, "Last night was a mistake. I don't want to give my life to Christ again!"

I was shocked! That was the first time I ever heard someone say that serving God was a mistake. No amount of words could change his mind.

This gentleman had obviously heard about the love of God but could not comprehend the breadth, depth, length, and height. It comes only by revelation! He valued the love of his girlfriend more than the love of God.

The extent to which you are convinced of someone's love will always determine the kind and type of favours you ask from the person. It is very easy for me to ask my wife for anything because I am convinced she loves me.

THE EFFECT OF UNDERSTANDING GOD'S LOVE

Now unto him that is *able to do exceeding abundantly above all* that *we ask or think*, according to the power that worketh in us (Eph. 3:20).

It is only when we have this revelation of the love of God that we can begin to pray for the unimaginable; things that are beyond our thinking and abilities. I believe we move into the zone of the miraculous. Our faith is charged and boldness enters our heart.

The store houses of heaven are filled with good things. It can be all yours if only you can deepen your understanding of the love of God.

Someone's breakthrough is lying in heaven right now! Someone's wife is standing in heaven right now! Someone's wedding gown has been sown already in heaven! Someone's car engine has been started by an angel in heaven right now! May you understand the love of God!

LOVE PRODUCES FAITH

For in Jesus Christ neither circumcision availeth any thing, nor uncircumcision; but *faith which worketh by love* (Gal. 5:6).

Love is a fuel that faith needs to work. I remember when I was a student. I had enough faith to sometimes borrow my wife's car because of the love I knew she had for me.

The more understanding you have about how much someone loves you, the more faith you will have toward the person.

I Want a Woman Who Can Spend Money

I once met a gentleman who told me he was looking for a wife.

"What kind of wife are you looking for?" I asked.

He replied, "I am looking for a woman who can spend money."

I was a little amazed, but he was serious.

When I asked him why, he answered, "If I find a woman who likes spending money, it will push me to make more money."

God is looking for someone who knows how to spend the grace of God. May you understand the love of God!

The Rule of the Name of Jesus

The Epileptic Child

The name of Jesus is the key to signs and wonders.

For to do whatsoever thy hand and thy counsel determined before to be done. And now, Lord, behold their threatenings: and grant unto thy servants, that with all boldness they may speak thy word, By stretching forth thine hand to heal; and that *signs and wonders* may be done *by the name of the holy child Jesus* (Acts 4:28-30).

One day a certain woman brought her epileptic child to me for healing. I took a bottle of anointing oil and prayed over him in faith, based on James 5:14-15a, which reads, "Is any sick among you? let him call for the elders of the church; and let them pray over him, anointing him with oil *in the name of the Lord*: and the prayer of faith shall save the sick." This means that the power is generated by the name of Jesus.

After about four months the mother came to see me. She said, "Prophet, from the day you prayed for my son, the epileptic attacks have ceased, and he is completely healed." That is the power behind the name of Jesus!

Nothing Happened When I Mentioned the Name of Jesus

Years ago when I was still a baby Christian I saw very few results when I prayed for people in the name of Jesus. This made me very worried. I used to ask myself, *What is wrong with me?*

Meanwhile, when others prayed I saw demons leave and healings, miracles, signs, and wonders occur. I wondered why nothing happened when I in particular mentioned the name of Jesus. It worried me because I had read all of these wonderful Scriptures about the power in the name.

Demons Can Mention the Name of Jesus

I remember once praying together with a group of pastors for a woman suffering from schizophrenia. Whenever the name of Jesus was mentioned, this woman would laugh out loud and repeat the name of Jesus in a mocking voice. I was very disturbed. Later on I discovered some people in the Bible who experienced a similar problem. Acts 19:15-16 says,

And the evil spirit answered and said, *Jesus I know, and Paul I know; but who are ye?* And the man in whom the evil spirit was leaped on them, and *overcame them*, and prevailed against them, so that they fled out of that house naked and wounded.

The name was only not working on him; he had the boldness to mention the name himself. Something was missing; something was failing to unlock the power in the name of Jesus.

THE NAME OF JESUS AND ANOTHER SPIRIT

Not every one that saith unto me, Lord, Lord, shall enter into the kingdom of heaven; but he that doeth the will of my Father which is in heaven. Many will say to me in that day, Lord, Lord, have we not *prophesied in thy name*? and in *thy name cast out devils*? And in thy name done many wonderful works? And then will I profess unto them, I never knew you: depart from me, ye that work iniquity (Matt. 7:21-23).

Jesus spoke about powerful ministers of God who will be turned away at the gates of heaven. This will include powerful prophets who prophesied and did wonderful works in His name. It will also include evangelists and apostles who had cast out devils and did many wonderful works. The interesting thing is, although they did all these wonderful things in the name of Jesus, He said He never knew them.

The word "never" means they were never associated with Jesus at any point in time. Translated into Greek, the word "never" is *oudepote*. It means not even at any time.

If Jesus was never associated with them, what power did they use to perform the miracles? If it was not the Holy Spirit, then it must have been another spirit operating under the guise of the name of Jesus.

Paul gave a warning about the probability of such a thing in his letter to the church of Corinth. Second Corinthians 11:4 reads,

For if he that cometh preacheth another Jesus, whom we have not preached, or if ye *receive another spirit*, which ye have not received, or another gospel, which ye have not accepted, ye might well bear with him.

It is possible to preach another Jesus with another gospel and another spirit other than the Holy Spirit.

CONDITIONS ATTACHED TO THE NAME OF JESUS

One day someone came to ask my permission to use my name concerning something he was doing. I spelled out certain conditions under which he could use my name; otherwise, I was not going to support what he was doing.

I believe the reason we sometimes do not seem to see the power associated with the name of Jesus is because there are several conditions we may have to meet. The same Jesus who said, "In My name shall they cast out devils," also gave several conditions attached to this name.

Ye have not chosen me, but I have chosen you, and ordained you, that ye should go and bring forth fruit, and that your fruit should remain: that *whatsoever ye shall ask of the Father in my name. he may give it you* (John 15:16).

The words "that whatsoever ye shall ask the Father in my name, he will give it to you" makes the use of the name conditional. Jesus spelled out some conditions attached to His name.

Let us examine some of the conditions in this verse. Three key conditional words must be noted: *chosen, ordained,* and *fruit.* We will be looking at these words in detail.

THE NAME AND THE WILL OF GOD

The name of Jesus will work on things God has chosen. In other words, it is effective when used in relation with God's "choices, will, plan, and initiative."

The word "initiative" means to take the first step. Otherwise I could pray in the name of Jesus that God should help me steal, but that will obviously not be God's will.

The name of Jesus did not work for the seven sons of Sceva because they were outside the will of God. They were not born again; neither were they sent by the Lord. They mentioned the name of Jesus, but it had no effect on the demons.

Your Choices Matter

Jesus made a comment about the right spiritual atmosphere for miracles.

And he that sent me is with me: the Father hath not left me alone; for *I do always those things that please him* (John 8:29).

He said, "The Holy Spirit is always with Me because I make sure I do the things that please God." Not the things that please me, my wife, or my boss, but the things that please Him. In other words, "I follow the will or choices of God for my life."

Jonah Was Not in the Will of God

In the book of Jonah, God sent Jonah to preach to the people of Nineveh. He disobeyed and instead took a ship to flee to Tarshish. God became angry with him and sent a great storm into the sea. The sailors and Jonah prayed that the storm would stop, but it did not abate. The prayers of Jonah were unanswered because he was outside the will of God.

THE NAME AND WHAT GOD HAS ORDAINED

When translated, the literal Greek meaning of the word "ordain" is *to place*. Another English definition of "ordain" is *to appoint*. There are two types of placement or appointment in our relationship with God: a spiritual placement and a physical placement. When we allow God to place us both spiritually and physically, it creates a conducive environment for answered prayer.

SPIRITUAL AND PHYSICAL PLACEMENT

Many years ago I had an experience with God that changed the entire course of my life forever. The Lord appeared to me in a vision and appointed me as a prophet and a teacher. I have seen the name of Jesus work many powerful miracles, signs, and wonders as I have operated within the boundaries of this appointment or calling. I believe physical placement also has a lot to do with answered prayer. You must be properly located in the right city, job, etc., as directed by the Lord.

The Name of Jesus Worked Powerfully for the Seventy

After these things the Lord appointed other seventy also, and sent them two and two before his face into every city and place, whither he himself would come (Luke 10:1).

The seventy Jesus sent out to preach enjoyed great success in ministry. This was because of placement. Spiritually they were well placed because they were chosen by Jesus—not man. Physically they were well placed because He showed them which cities to visit. The result was prayer backed with signs and wonders.

They came back with a report, saying, "Lord, even the devils are subject unto us through thy name" (Luke 10:17b).

What have you been appointed to do? Do it and see your prayer life thrive.

My Own Experience

When I finished my first degree, I went to America with the view to continue with my postgraduate degree. The Lord Jesus appeared to me and asked me to leave because that was not the place He had appointed for me. He also reminded me I was supposed to be in the ministry. I immediately obeyed this vision concerning my physical and spiritual placement.

I wonder what would have happened if I had disobeyed. I believe the Lord would have still been with me, but it would have been difficult to have a very successful prayer life, as I have now, because I would have been operating outside the will of God.

The Example of Paul

And it came to pass, that, when I was come again to Jerusalem, even while I prayed in the temple, I was in a trance; And saw him saying unto me, *Make haste, and get thee quickly out of Jerusalem*: for they will not receive thy testimony concerning me (Acts 22:17-18).

Paul was instructed by the Lord concerning his spiritual placement. He was to leave Jerusalem and preach the Gospel to the Gentiles.

It would not have mattered how hard he would have prayed in the name of Jesus. If Paul had persisted in having his ministry in Jerusalem, he would have borne very little fruit. This is because he would have been operating outside God's placement.

THE NAME AND "FRUIT"

But the fruit of the Spirit is *love, joy, peace, longsuffering, gentleness, goodness, faith, meekness, temperance*: against such there is no law (Gal. 5:22-23).

It is important we bear spiritual fruit if we are to have a powerful prayer life. Jesus said, "You should go and bring forth fruit that whatsoever you may ask the Father in My name, He will give it to you."

I want to break the fruit into two categories: our relationship with others and our relationship with God. This is important because this is closely connected with the law of relationships, which I mentioned earlier. Without a good relationship with God and man, your prayer can be greatly hindered.

1. Fruit and Our Relationship with Others

Therefore if thou bring thy gift to the altar, and there rememberest that thy brother hath ought against thee; Leave there thy gift before the altar, and go thy way; first be reconciled to thy brother, and then come and offer thy gift (Matt. 5:23-24).

Spiritual fruit have to do largely with our *character* and *nature*. We are usually forced to bear this fruit as we relate to other people. Love, longsuffering, gentleness, goodness, and meekness are usually borne in the soil of relationships.

Relationships expose our weaknesses and test our strengths. It forces us to work on the weak areas of our character. For example, marriage requires temperance or self-control. It can force you to control your emotions as you try to build a better relationship with your spouse.

Relationships can test our strength because when you are strong in a particular area, it will take longsuffering and gentleness to deal with people who may not be as intelligent as you are. It is important to bear fruits because one condition of answered prayer is having a harmonious relationship with other people. The development of these fruits helps us meet that requirement.

I believe the reason divorce is on the increase is because we are not longsuffering. This has resulted in many broken homes. "Longsuffering" literally means to suffer for long. The only way to develop it is by suffering for long.

"Meekness," on the other hand, means "being humble to the Word of God." When the Bible says, "Do not commit adultery or fornication," we must be humble enough to obey.

"Temperance" means "self-control." Even when we are angry, we must be able to control ourselves and not hurl swear words and insults.

When you borrow someone's money, be sure to pay it back. These things grieve the Holy Spirit. You should not only bring forth fruit, but your fruit should remain, not just for a week, but for a long time.

2. Fruit and Our Relationship with God

When we relate with God by prayer, the Word, and holiness, we produce the fruit of *love, joy, peace,* and *faith.* The name of Jesus will work when we have *faith.*

In Acts 3:16, the Bible says, "And *his name through faith in his name* hath made this man strong, whom ye see and know: yea, the faith which is by him hath given him this perfect soundness in the presence of you all."

Do you know why demons can mention the name? Because when they mention it, there is no faith behind it. It takes faith to activate the power in the name! Our faith grows as we study God's Word and relate to Him.

For example, when a doctor is performing a surgery, you may think he has just cut a portion of a patient's skin. But in his mind he has opened about ten medical books that you cannot see. That action may look like a simple procedure, but that procedure is based on years of study and experience.

It is the same with prayer. When I am praying, for instance, I just say a few simple words. But in my heart I may have opened many Scriptures in my spirit that you cannot see. You may think it is a simple procedure, but it is a complex one. It is those Scriptures that generate the faith needed to work miracles.

THE NAME OF JESUS AND REVELATION

Ephesians 1:18-21 says,

The eyes of your understanding being enlightened; that ye may know what is the hope of his calling, and what the riches of the glory of his inheritance in the saints, And what is the exceeding greatness of his power to us-ward who believe, according to the working of his mighty power, Which he wrought in Christ, when he raised him from the dead, and set him at his own right hand in the heavenly places. Far above all principality, and power, and might, and dominion, and every name that is named, not only in this world, but also in that which is to come.

Paul prayed for the church in Ephesus to have revelation in three areas: *their calling*; *the riches of His glory*; and *the power of God*. Concerning the power of God, he emphasized that the church would have a revelation about the name of Jesus.

There are different ways you can know things. You can know them intellectually, experientially, or spiritually. Sometimes when we read something from the Scripture, we may know it mentally but not spiritually.

Revelation is understanding and knowing things by your spirit. That was why Jesus said to Simon Peter, "Flesh and blood has not revealed this to you." In other words, you did not know this mentally. When we have a revelation about the name of Jesus, we will have access to the exceeding great power of God.

My Search

Years ago as a young minister I became frustrated by the lack of power, signs, and wonders in my ministry. I embarked on a scriptural and spiritual search to find answers as to why I was not working miracles with the name of Jesus. I bought many books about the name of Jesus. I also used my Bible and concordance to read Scriptures concerning the name of Jesus. At certain periods I combined this with prayer and fasting.

Then one day something happened. I was praying in my room when I was suddenly caught up in the Spirit and saw the heavens open. I saw someone like Jesus descending from the clouds. I also saw many angels clothed in white, singing, "Hail the Lord, hail the Lord." Then I saw Jesus walking in the midst of them. I said, "Jesus is coming." I felt a great power and presence in my room. Then I fell down to worship.

When He came and stood before me, something told me to lift up my head and look at Him. I noticed there was something odd about His clothes; they were not shining. I have seen Jesus before and His garments radiated with light, but this time there was no brilliance. I wondered why.

When I looked at Him, my eyes locked with two green eyes. I immediately knew this was not Jesus. I was looking at Satan, eyeball to eyeball. The devil was standing there.

Second Corinthians 11:14-15 says, "And no marvel; for Satan himself is transformed into an angel of light. Therefore it is no great thing if his ministers also be transformed as the ministers of righteousness; whose end shall be according to their works."

The fear that gripped my heart was unexplainable. Then I screamed, "Jesus!" Suddenly, I heard a loud explosion, "Boooooom!" All of a sudden a bright light flashed in the room. Satan and his angels were blown away by the name of Jesus.

Then the Lord said to me, "My son, you wanted to know about the name of Jesus. Today I have given you a revelation about the power behind

The Rule of the Name of Jesus

that name. When you pray, you will see My name at work."

You don't need to have this same experience to understand and know the power behind the name of Jesus. God will only have to grant you a revelation in your spirit.

It is not everything that a man can teach you. Some things can be taught by God alone. Jesus said to His disciples, "I have yet many things to say unto you, but ye cannot bear them now. Howbeit when he, the Spirit of truth, is come, he will guide you into all truth: for he shall not speak of himself; but whatsoever he shall hear, that shall he speak: and he will shew you things to come" (John 16:12-13). Even Jesus could not teach everything. He said the Holy Spirit will teach you the rest.

I would like you to lift up your hands and pray that God will open the eyes of your understanding and enlighten you about the power in the name of Jesus.

Father, I pray for Your child. I pray You grant Your child a revelation about the name of Jesus. Amen!

The White Horse

Any time I read the book of Revelation, I feel as if I am watching a scene in a Hollywood movie because most of the things look surreal. You know, heaven will be an interesting place to be. We can never get bored because it seems even the image of God is not constant; it changes.

Sometimes Jesus appears as a man with His hair as white as wool and eyes shining with light. In another place you see Him as a lamb that was slain; and the next time you see Him, He is on a horse with swords coming out of His mouth. What excitement!

THE NAMES OF JESUS

And I saw heaven opened, and behold a white horse; and he that sat upon him was called *Faithful* and *True*, and in *righteousness* he doth judge and make war. His eyes were as a flame of fire, and on his head were many crowns; and he had a name written, that no man knew, but he himself. And he was clothed with a vesture dipped in blood: and his name is called The Word of God. And the armies which were in heaven followed him upon white horses, clothed in fine linen, white and clean. And out of his mouth goeth a sharp sword, that with it he should smite the nations: and he shall rule them with a rod of iron: and he treadeth the winepress of the fierceness and wrath of Almighty God. And he hath on his vesture and on his thigh a name written, King Of Kings, And Lord Of Lords (Rev. 19:11-16).

Some of the names of Jesus mentioned in the Scripture above are the *Word of God, King of Kings,* and *Lord of Lords*. Most people have at least two names but some have even more. In the same way Jesus has several names. John called Him the *Word of God*. That is the name Jesus was referred to before His incarnation on earth.

John 1:1 says, "In the beginning was *the Word*, and the Word was with God, and the Word was God. Verse 14 says, "And the Word was made flesh, and dwelt among us, (and we beheld his glory, the glory as of the only begotten of the Father,) full of grace and truth."

WHAT MAKES THE NAME OF JESUS POWERFUL?

The Word of God, also known as *Jesus*, is the one seen sitting on the white horse. I would like you to notice that the name of Jesus is supported by *armies* and *weapons*.

There is an army in heaven that enforces what He, the Word of God, says. For example, the US president may look like any other human being, but make no mistake; behind his words are armies and weapons that can move at his command. When he says, "Attack," behind that word are nuclear bombs, submarines, machine guns, and army personnel. Similarly, the name of Jesus is supported by spiritual armies and weapons!

WHAT DOES IT TAKE TO RELEASE THE ARMY?

And I saw heaven opened, and behold a white horse; and he that sat upon him was called *Faithful* and *True*, and in *righteousness* . . . (Rev. 19:11).

Jesus, who was leading the army, sat on a white horse. He is able to lead this army because of three qualities He possesses: *Faithfulness, Truthfulness*, and *Righteousness*. I believe this has lessons for us to learn. To have the backing army of heaven in prayer, you will need these qualities.

Vision of the White Horse

A brother once shared a supernatural experience he had with me. He was lying on his bed,

The White Horse

listening to an audio message I had preached about an encounter I had with Jesus. He began to pray and asked God for a supernatural experience because he had never had one before. Suddenly a white horse appeared at his bedside. The horse spoke and told him he had been sent by the Lord to bring him to heaven in response to his prayer. He was speechless.

When he mounted the horse its colour changed from pure white to grey. He asked the horse, "Why has your colour changed?"

The horse replied, "I portray the holiness of the person who sits on me; I become darker when you are more sinful."

He bowed his head in shame. You need a particular spiritual quality to mount the white horse.

1. FAITHFUL

The word "faithful" means *loyal*. Loyal to whom? To God and His Word! One of the things that tests your loyalty is *time*.

In Matthew 25 the Bible talks about the parable of the talents. In verse 19 it says, "*After a long time* the lord of those servants cometh, and reckoneth with them."

This is one of the things that make marriage, for example, difficult; the passage of time.

Short-term relationships are easy to manage because they don't expose you to different seasons of life.

For example, being in a relationship with someone you met six months ago is different from being in that same relationship after ten years of marriage. The person may have changed radically by putting on a lot of weight. The person may be suffering from low sperm count and now cannot have a baby. This new season can challenge the marriage.

Serving God as a student is different from serving God as a married person. Serving God as a rich person is different from serving God as someone who is broke. Because of this, many people find it difficult to be consistent in their walk with God. The seasons expose weaknesses which hitherto were hidden and untested.

Hebrews 3:1-2 says, "Wherefore, holy brethren, partakers of the heavenly calling, consider the Apostle and High Priest of our profession, Christ Jesus; Who was *faithful to him* that appointed him, as also Moses was faithful in all his house."

Do you know what this means? Jesus was sent forth from God to earth as an apostle to represent God and later went to heaven as a high priest to represent us. But whether on earth or in heaven, He was faithful. A change in status, location, and position did not change Him.

I have seen people backslide because of money. Luke 16:11 says, "If therefore ye have *not been faithful* in the unrighteous mammon, who will commit to your trust the true riches?" If you attend every prayer meeting and you are not faithful to God, it can undermine your prayer. The army may not respond. A powerful prayer life is generated by your lifestyle!

Matthew 25:23 states, "*Well done, good and faithful servant*; thou hast been faithful over a few things, I will make thee ruler over many things: enter thou into the joy of thy lord."

Faithfulness changed the status of that servant from a servant to a ruler. When we are faithful to God and His Word, we will rule in prayer.

2. TRUE

The word "true" means *genuine*. You know, it is amazing how things in the natural realm seem to mirror the spirit realm. The natural realm is truly a manifestation of the spiritual. Increasingly it is becoming difficult to distinguish between the real and the fake in this world.

The Fake Dog

Someone once sold a dog to me, which he claimed was an exotic breed. In fact, under normal circumstances I would not have taken that particular man at his word. But because he was introduced to me by a church member I gave him the benefit of the doubt. Later the dog failed to develop all the features associated with that type of dog. Finally I came to the conclusion that it was fake! I called the man and asked him to come for his dog.

In the same manner God is waiting for some Christians to bear the fruit of the Spirit. Unfortunately, over time they have failed to develop the features associated with Christianity. Do you know what that means? They are fake! The time has come for you to be a genuine Christian because the army and weapons behind the name of Jesus respond to people who are true.

3. RIGHTEOUS

The word "righteous" means *holy*. The only thing the devil cannot copy is holiness. He can copy signs, miracles, power, etc.

When Jesus entered the temple in Luke 4:34, the evil spirit said to Him, "I know thee who thou art; the *Holy One of God*." What gave power to His name was holiness. The evil spirit knew that a combination of the name of Jesus and holiness is a dangerous cocktail.

Dear reader, it is not a question of just rushing to every prayer meeting. It is a question of knowing the rules of engagement. Let's be faithful, let's be true, and let's be righteous; and when we pray with the name of Jesus, the armies of heaven will respond to us. May heaven respond to your prayers!

About the Author

Kakra Baiden

MANY YEARS AGO the Lord Jesus Christ appeared in a vision to Kakra Baiden and called him into the ministry as a prophet, teacher, and miracle worker. He is also known as "the walking Bible" for his supernatural ability to preach and teach the Bible from memory.

Pastor Baiden is an architect by profession and serves as a bishop of the Lighthouse Chapel International denomination. He has trained many pastors and planted many churches within the Lighthouse denomination.

Currently he is the senior pastor of the Morning Star Cathedral, Lighthouse Chapel International, Accra. He is a sought-after revivalist and conference speaker.

He is also the president of Airpower, a ministry through which he touches the world through radio and TV broadcasts, books, CDs, videos, the Internet, and international conferences dubbed "The Airpower Conference." He has ministered the Word on every continent and is also the author of the best-selling book, *Squatters*.

Pastor Baiden is married to Lady Rev. Dr. Ewuradwoa Baiden and they have four children.

For additional information on Kakra Baiden's books and messages (CDs and DVDs), write to any of these addresses:

US

26219 Halbrook Glen Lane
Katy, TX 77494

UK

32 Tern Road
Hampton, Hargate
Cambridgeshire
Pe78DG

GHANA

P.O. Box SK 1067
Sakumono Estates, Tema
Ghana-West Africa

E-MAIL: info@kakrabaiden.org

WEBSITE: www.kakrabaiden.org

FACEBOOK: www.facebook.com/KakraBaiden

TWITTER: www.twitter.com/ProphetKakraB

CONTACT NUMBERS:
+233 273 437 440 / +233 249 217 272 /
+233 207575215

www.ingramcontent.com/pod-product-compliance
Lightning Source LLC
Chambersburg PA
CBHW060424050426
42449CB00009B/2120